DIY House Cleaning Hacks

70+ Cleaning Hacks For Stress-Free Cleaning

Mathew Stone

Copyright © 2014 by Mathew Stone. All rights reserved.

No part of this book can be reproduced in any way or by any means, electronic or mechanical, including recording or photocopying, or by any other means without permission in writing from the author.

While the author has made all attempts to verify the information offered in this publication, neither the author nor the publisher assumes any responsibility for errors, omissions, or contrary interpretations of the subject matter herein.

The views expressed in this book are those of the author alone and should not be taken as expert commands or instructions. The reader of this book assumes full responsibility for their own actions.

Neither the author nor the publisher assumes any responsibility or liability whatsoever on behalf of the reader or purchaser of this content.

BONUS

7 Things You Have Probably Overlooked or Forgotten to Clean

Thank You For Downloading This Book! Please jump to the bottom of this book to read your bonus!

Table of Contents

The "Pro Cleaning" Mindset
Living With The "Pro Cleaning Mindset": The Golden Rules
The "Six Most Important" Cleaning Hacks
DIY Cleaning Hacks for the Kitchen: Time to Beat the Grime
DIY Bathroom Cleaning Hacks
DIY Bedroom Cleaning Hacks
DIY Cleaning Hacks For The Living Room
Homemade Cleaning Products
Bathroom Cleaners
Tub And Tile Cleanser
Scouring Powder
Toilet Bowl Cleaner
Glass Cleaner
Glass Cleaner
Floor Sanitizer
Soap Scum Remover
Calcium Or Lime Deposit Remover
Mold Or Mildew Remover
Tub Scrub
DIY Kitchen Cleaning Products
All Purpose Cleanser
Freshen Your Garbage Disposal
Sinks And Stovetop Cleanser
Homemade Wood Polish
Stain Patrol
Red Wine Stains
Coffee Stains

Other Stains
DIY Laundry Detergents, Fabric Softeners and Clothing Refreshers
Fabric Softener Ideas
Clothes Freshener
Snow Can Clean Your Rug
THANKYOU BONUS- 7 Things You Have Probably Overlooked or Forgotten to Clean

The "Pro Cleaning" Mindset

If you're reading this book, you're definitely a devoted homemaker who is willing to be perfect in all aspects of life, be it looking after kids or completing household chores efficiently.

If you want to make the most of the tips, tricks and hacks in this home cleaning guide, you'll have to adopt the "pro cleaning mindset". So, if you're someone who prefers leaving things until the very last minute, it's time to change your mindset.

Imagine this...

You're watching your favourite TV show and your kid spills some fruit juice on your carpet. Thinking that you'll take care of the stain later, you keep watching TV and end up scrubbing the carpet for 10-15 minutes later on.

But, if you were living with the "pro cleaning mindset", you would have cleaned the carpet immediately, which would barely take 5-7 seconds.

So, the "pro cleaning mindset" is all about taking the right immediate actions to keep small chores from snowballing into bigger troubles.

Living With The "Pro Cleaning Mindset": The Golden Rules

Rule # 1: It's Now Or Never

As a homemaker, you need to promise yourself that you will not ignore or delay any household chore that takes less than two-three minutes to complete. Whether it's picking up a toy from the floor or wiping spilled juice, take action IMMEDIATELY.

Rule # 2: No Breaks In The Middle

When you're working on a chore, don't take a break unless you've finished it completely. Trust me, it's really difficult to come back and focus on tasks like kitchen cabinet cleaning if you leave them in the middle.

Rule # 3: Consistent Cleaning Matters

As a cleaning pro, your goal should be cleaning things as you go. Whether it's a plate on the dinner table or the milk jug that you've just taken out of the refrigerator, don't let the mess pile up.

When it comes to putting things back in their position, be as quick and vigilant as possible. You may feel like dozing off after a long day of work, but sorting and putting away that laundry pile would definitely keep mess from building up.

Rule # 4: Stick With Your Cleaning Plan

I prefer leaving tedious cleaning chores for a special day in the week. For example, you could deep-clean the bedroom, kitchen or living room on Mondays and take care of regular household chores on a daily basis.

Make a plan that works best for you and stick with it.

Rule # 5: Set Cleaning Rules For All

Of course, the job of a homemaker is to maintain a well-organized and clean house. But, that doesn't mean that you'll be cleaning all day and picking up your children's toys from time to time.

To maintain a clean, well-organized and happy home, you must take out some time for your hobbies, your interests and your social life. So, here's the plan. Set some rules for everyone in your home and make sure that everyone follows them.

For example, your kids should know that they have to pick up the playroom before lunch, they need to have their plates taken to the counter, and they have to dump their dirty clothes in the special laundry hamper.

Rule # 6: The Earlier The Better

The earlier you get done with household chores, the more time you can invest in your favourite activities throughout the day. I prefer finishing major household chores in the morning so I have time for other things during the day.

Rule # 7: Patience Is Virtue

Whether it is getting excellent and consistent results from your regular household chores or making your kids used to the new cleaning rules you've set, be patient. Change will happen, but it won't occur overnight.

Rule # 8: It's My Home, It's My Responsibility

Sometimes, piled up mess may make you lose your cool, and you may be frustrated with all the work you've to do every day. But, don't use it as an excuse to leave your home the way it is.

Whether you're a stay-at-home Dad or a busy working Mom, always remember that it's your home, and it is your responsibility.

Housekeeping ain't no joke. —Louisa May Alcott

The "Six Most Important" Cleaning Hacks

There are very few people who can honestly say that cleaning is their favorite thing to do but many people make it harder on themselves than it needs to be.

They are spending extra time and energy on cleaning things that do not need to be fussed with or are running back and forth because they have not developed an easy to follow cleaning plan.

There are several things that you can do for your

general house cleaning that will make the process faster and easier.

Even if you do not follow all of these tips, you will find one or two that will save you a great deal of time. Read these tips before moving on to the more room-specific cleaning tips and tricks that I have in store for you.

Tip #1: Clean As You Go

If you wait until that "perfect" moment to clean, you will be faced with a gigantic mess to deal with and very little time to get everything done.

There are plenty of chances for you to use this tip in every room of your house: clean the shower while you are finishing up- everything is already wet so all you need is a few flicks of the soapy cloth or a hidden shower squeegee and you are done.

Hang clothes back in the closet as you are dressing- or throw them directly into the hamper as you remove them. If you have clothes that will need to go to the dry cleaner, toss them in a separate basket that is used just for that purpose.

Tip # 2: Keep Everything In The Right Room

Do you know why people are supposed to eat in the kitchen? Because the surfaces in that room are specially designed for eating, which makes them easier to clean when the time comes.

If you are eating in your bedroom, you are not only eating in a room not equipped with the right surface, but you are potentially inviting pests and critters into the room as well.

Tip # 3: Practice Prevention As Much As Possible

Once dirt is in your house, you have to deal with it. If you keep more dirt outside that is less dirt that you have to deal with, get the picture?

Ban shoes from the house to keep from bringing dirt in and close the windows when there is construction or other dirt producers at work.

Tip # 4: Practice Efficiency

If you are running from room to room doing a bit here and bit there, you are wasting your time and energy. You will never finish a whole room before you end up utterly exhausted and disgusted with how little progress you are making.

Make up a little basket of cleaning supplies including solutions that work on several surfaces, clean rags and a trash bag and bring the basket with you from room to room as you go. Finish one room at a time.

Tip # 5: Avoid This: You Never Set A Schedule For Your Cleaning, You Just Hope For The Right Time To Come Along

Here is a major hint: the "right" time is never going to come along, especially for a chore that you truly hate. Instead of waiting around for that moment or hoping for random times to come up, block off a period of time to clean a room or a particular area and then stick to that schedule.

Tip # 6: You Forget To Make It More Fun

Yes, cleaning can actually be enjoyable if you do it correctly. Blast your favorite upbeat music or watch a show while you are cleaning.

Listen to an audio book and get smart while you are getting clean.

Do something that you enjoy while you are doing something that you truly do not and it will all balance out.

DIY Cleaning Hacks For The Kitchen: Time To Beat The Grime

* Pyrex and heavy roasting pans can be cleaned with your regular oven cleaning products. Remember: the fumes can be toxic so make sure that you are using these types of cleaners in a well-ventilated area and use gloves to protect your hands.

* Heavy pans can also be cleaned by putting them in the oven during the self-cleaning cycle. Do not try this with thinner pans as they can warp.

* Make it a habit to put your kitchen sponges in the dishwasher whenever it is run to keep them from growing bacteria .

* Clean your reusable bottles, narrow vases and other hard to clean items with a denture tablet or two and some water. The tablets will loosen any gunk and you can just rinse it all away. This will also work for mugs and teacups that are stained with coffee or tea.

* To clean copper: mix three parts of ordinary flour with one part salt and then add enough regular vinegar to make a nice paste. Apply the paste and then let sit for thirty minutes before rinsing thoroughly. This works for silver as well.

Another option for both copper and silver is non-gel toothpaste.

* A stained coffee carafe will come sparkling clean with minimal effort with nothing more than some salt and some ice cubes. Put the ice and salt in the carafe and give it a few good swirls and the stains will just be whisked away.

* Since you cannot wash champagne glasses with soap there are two options. Either run them through the dishwasher on high heat without soap or wash them by hand being careful to keep any soap on the outside only.

* Clean stainless steel appliances in your kitchen with ordinary flour- just apply the flour with a

clean cloth and buff the surface clean. Wipe the newly cleaned surface with a second clean cloth and you will get a finger print-free surface as well.

* One of the worst areas of the kitchen to clean is the stove top and the stove hood because of all of the accumulated grease and grime there. While it might seem counterproductive, oil is your best friend here. Dab some mineral or vegetable oil on the surface of the grime and allow it to set for a few minutes.

This oil will break down the old oil and allow it to be more easily lifted and removed. Once you have the surface cleaned ,once again use a very thin layer of additional oil to prevent future build up.

* Getting rid of the gunk on your stove top's burners can be a headache.

To make this task easier, find a set of bags with tight seals large enough to hold each burner. Put the burner into each bag and then add in about a quarter of a cup of straight ammonia and then quickly seal the bag.

Put the sealed bags in a bucket or the sink in case they leak and then leave them overnight. All of the burned on gunk should just rinse away.

* To easily clean your microwave, you will need a microwaveable bowl, two tablespoons of vinegar and some water. Run the microwave on high for about five minutes and the steam will soften and

loosen even the toughest food splatters, allowing them to be easily and quickly wiped away.

* Dinner got away from you and now there is burned food stuck to the bottom of your pan. Before you panic and toss the pan into the trash, here is what you do.

First, using a wooden or plastic spoon, scrape out as much of the gunk as you can. Next, fill the pan a quarter of the way full. Add several tablespoons of baking soda to the pan and then boil for fifteen minutes.

Whatever is left in the pan should come right out. For a really badly burned pan, you may have to repeat this process a time or two.

*A mixture of baking soda and salt can be used to clean virtually any surface in your home, not just your kitchen.

* Salt and half of a lemon can be used to clean and deodorize your wooden cutting boards. Sprinkle the board with the salt first, and then use the cut lemon to scrub the salt into the surface.

* Cream of tartar mixed with enough water to make a thin paste is especially good for cleaning stainless steel.

* To clean your cast iron skillets, use olive oil and

salt. Everyone knows that you cannot use soap on cast iron- so use a mixture of olive oil and salt to scour the pan out and then finish with a thin coating of olive oil before storing.

DIY Bathroom Cleaning Hacks

* Leave a small opening at the ends of the shower curtain or shower door to keep the air flowing and to cut down on mildew. If your family will flood out the floor, this will encourage them to open the door or curtain all the way after their shower to allow it to air out and then close them so that no mold can grow in the folds of the curtain.

* Use black tea to clean the bathroom mirror. Just wipe the freshly brewed tea onto the mirror with a clean cloth and then buff dry.

* Use a mixture of vinegar and baking soda in the

toilet bowl to get it sparkling clean with minimal effort. Simply dump in the baking soda and then add a few tablespoons of vinegar. Don't worry, this mixture will foam up.

Leave it set for fifteen minutes or so and you are set. (This mixture also works well to unclog bathtub and sink drains as well.)

* Wipe your sink and tub fixtures with a little bit of oil on a soft cloth and they will sparkle like brand new.

* When you get new cans of products that you leave on the side of the sink or tub, paint them with clear nail polish to prevent the rust rings from forming.

* You can use a cut grapefruit and some salt to clean your bathtub. You can also use a lemon and cream of tartar in the same way.

* If you are finding that your shower curtain no longer glides along the curtain rod like it is supposed to, spread a thin layer of petroleum jelly on the rod as lubrication. You can use hair conditioner or body lotion to do this and softly scent the room in the process if you prefer.

* Another very odd tip: use non-stick cooking spray on your shower walls and the grime will not get a chance to stick to any surface. Caution: this spray makes the bathtub surface very slippery so use cautiously.

* You can use a dryer sheet to clean a glass shower door.

* If you rub bar soap on a bathroom mirror and then buff with a soft cloth the mirror will stay fog free for several days at a time. You can also do this with shaving cream.

* If you notice that your shower head is spraying in all the wrong places or the water pressure seems to be a little iffy, you might have hard water deposits. To clean the shower head and get it working like new once again, you will need a plastic bag and some ordinary vinegar.

Put the plastic bag over the shower head and fill with vinegar. Tie the bag closed and leave on overnight. (You can also take the shower head off and do the same thing if you prefer.)

DIY Bedroom Cleaning Hacks

* Carpets and upholstered furniture should be kept to a minimum here. If you can't get rid of them altogether, then invest in a very good vacuum cleaner so that you can minimize dust and dander.

* Clean the bedroom at least once a week, including wiping down all surfaces with a damp cloth.

* Wash the curtains (if they are washable) if they are not, then vacuum or steam clean them frequently. If you must dry clean your curtains then do so when it is time to change them for the season

so that you are storing clean curtains.

* Do not leave clothes on the floor- either put them away or directly into the hamper.

* There should be a solid no shoes allowed in the bedroom rule in your home.

* Air out the bedroom whenever you get a chance to do so.

* Install HEPA filters especially in the bedroom vent.

* Consider a dehumidifier in the bedroom because

dust mites absolutely thrive where it is warm and humid.

* Keep pets out of the bedroom especially if you are sensitive or have allergies.

*Use an adhesive lint roller to dust your lamp shades. You can also use a blow dryer set on "cool" to blow the dust from the shade.

* If you spill something oily on your carpet, do not panic. First, soak up as much of the oil as you can. Then, sprinkle the remaining stain with cornstarch or baking soda and allow to set for ten to fifteen minutes.

In the meantime, mix two cups of warm water, one tablespoon of clear dish detergent and one tablespoon of regular vinegar. Vacuum the cornstarch or baking soda up and then use the water mixture to dab at the stain.

Tips Specifically For Your Bed

* Use a mattress and box spring cover that is both dust and allergen proof.

* Do not use any item on your bed that is not machine washable.

Bedroom Furniture Tip

* It is better to keep furniture here at a minimum. If you can avoid upholstery, do so.

DIY Cleaning Hacks for the Living Room

* Pick up items as you go- put the living room items away as you go and everything else into a container that will be dealt with when you are finished. (If there are toys in the living room then make the children do a small chore to earn back their toys.)

* Brush off the couch cushions on both sides. Sweep the dirt from under the couch cushions to the floor. Collect the sixty seven cents in loose change that you find there. Fluff up and arrange the pillows.

* Wipe off the coffee table and then stack the books or magazines there in a tidy pile.

* Sweep or vacuum the main parts of the floor.

* Repair scratches on the wood floor or furniture as you are working. You can either use specially designed wood markers or you can use crayons to color in the scratches. Buff with a cloth and you are done.

* Simple cleaning for your window blinds. Instead of taking the blinds down and then struggling to get them back in place, use water and vinegar and a pair of old but clean socks. Mix the water and

vinegar in a fifty/fifty ratio.

With one sock worn on your hand like a glove, wipe down the blinds using your cleaning mixture. Use the other sock to dry the blinds. Either throw the socks away or wash them for the next cleaning day.

Homemade Cleaning Products

Simpler to use than the store-bought varieties, homemade cleaners are better for you, your home and the environment. Many of the following cleaners can be used on many other surfaces in other rooms than are listed.

Bathroom Cleaners

You will need:

* Baking soda, which is used to clean, deodorize and scour

* Borax: a cleanser, deodorizer, disinfectant and will also help repel some insects as well. (Borax is also used for laundry.)

* Castile or vegetable oil based liquid soap.

* White vinegar, which is used to cut soap scum and grease, dissolve mineral deposits, kill bacteria, inhibit the growth of mold and viruses on surfaces.

* Essential oils: used to help freshen areas. Some are antibacterial as well.

* Kosher salt is used to scour and disinfect.

You will also need jars and spray bottles to keep your mixtures in and to help you to use them. Some of the cleaners you will create can be kept for up to a year while others will only be enough for one-time cleaning.

For A Tub And Tile Cleanser

Mix 1 2/3 cup of baking soda with ½ cup of the liquid soap plus ½ cup of water and 2 tablespoons of vinegar. Shake the mixture well and then apply with a sponge or damp cloth. Rinse the surface well with plain water.

Scouring Powder

Mix one cup each baking soda, borax and kosher salt. Sprinkle your powder on the surface that you are cleaning and then wipe off. Rinse well with clear water and then dry with an additional cloth.

Toilet Bowl Cleaner

Mix ¼ cup of borax (you can also use baking soda here if you do not have borax on hand) and one cup of vinegar. Leave alone for 15 minutes or longer then use the toilet brush to loosen any tough stains. Flush the toilet and you are done.

Glass Cleaner

Mix ¼ cup of the vinegar with four cups of warm water and apply with a lint free cloth or a piece of newspaper.

Drain Cleaner

Better than the commercial drain cleaners because this will not damage your pipes and is not as toxic to humans. Dump ½ cup of baking soda into the drain followed by one cup of vinegar. This will foam up a lot but don't worry, it is supposed to do that.

Leave this alone for 15 minutes or so and then flush with hot or boiling water. The drain should be cleared out but if it is not, repeat the process a time or two. You can also use this tip to keep drains running better before they become blocked up in the first place.

Floor Sanitizer

Mix ½ cup of borax to two gallons of hot water in your mop bucket. Using a mop or a sponge, apply mixture to your floor. You do not need to rinse this off.

Soap Scum Remover

Plain baking soda on a cloth or sponge followed by a good rinse with clear water. You can also use kosher salt or vinegar to remove soap scum.

Calcium Or Lime Deposit Remover

If you have calcium or lime deposits on your faucets, just soak a towel in the white vinegar and then wrap it around the fixtures. Leave this on overnight and then remove the towel. The deposits should be completely gone.

Mold Or Mildew Remover

Mix ½ cup of borax with ½ cup of vinegar (more or less) to make a thick paste. Using a brush or a sponge, apply this to the areas and then rinse well. You may also apply the paste to the affected areas and leave for several hours before rinsing.

Tub Scrub

Mix one cup of baking soda with about ½ cup of castile soap. The mixture should look light and fluffy. At this point, you can add in five to ten drops of your favorite essential oil if you choose to. This mixture can be kept in a clearly labeled jar for up to one year.

DIY Kitchen Cleaning Products

Like the cleansers for the bathroom, many of these can transition to other surfaces. In fact, many of these cleansers can be used interchangeably for any room of the home.

You will need:

Lemons

Olive oil

Vinegar

Baking soda

Dish soap

Essential oils (these are optional)

An All Purpose Cleanser

1 teaspoon of baking soda, ½ teaspoon of baking soda and two tablespoons of vinegar. Add these to a spray bottle and shake.

Let the mixture settle down and then add enough water to fill the bottle.

If you want, you can add essential oils to this cleanser to give it a pleasant scent.

To Freshen Your Garbage Disposal

Save lemon or orange rinds while you are cooking and then grind them in the disposal with plenty of hot, running water.

Sinks And Stovetop Cleanser

Mix 1/3 cup of baking soda with enough water to form a thick paste. Scrub the paste onto the surface to be cleaned with a damp cloth and then buff dry.

Homemade Wood Polish For All Of Your Wooden Furniture

You will need:

The juice from one half of a lemon

About 1 tablespoon of olive oil

1 tablespoon of water

Add these three ingredients into a jar with a tightly fitting lid and then shake until they are all well blended. With a soft cloth, buff your wooden furniture with this mixture.

You must make this at the time that you are going to use it because it will go rancid very quickly. Once you are finished with the mixture, you must discard it.

Stain Patrol

Stains are sometimes unavoidable in the home- but you can get rid of some of the worst offenders with these tips.

Be warned: Not every stain can be removed and it is important to test combinations (even all natural ones) before you use them because they could make the problem even worse.

For A Red Wine Spill

A mixture of hydrogen peroxide and dish soap can be a life-saver. Blot as much of the stain up as possible and then squirt the dish soap mixed with the hydrogen peroxide directly onto it.

Allow this to set for several minutes and then start blotting with a clean, white towel. (Use a white towel so that you do not accidentally add a whole new color to the stain that you are trying to get rid of).

This mixture can work for ink stains as well.

Coffee Stains

Mix one egg yolk plus warm water until frothy and then pour directly onto the stain.

Any Other Stain

Mix ½ cup of dish detergent or shampoo with ½ cup of warm water using a hand mixer or a small blender to get it good and frothy.

DIY Laundry Detergents, Fabric Softeners and Clothing Refreshers

Homemade laundry detergent is a better alternative to store-bought laundry detergent that not only works very well but will save you tons of money in the long run as well.

What you will need:

1 bar of laundry soap. You can find these in the detergent aisle at most stores. You will grate this bar of soap into small pieces.

1 full box of borax. Again, this is usually found in the detergent aisle.

1 box of washing soda or baking soda. Washing soda might be found in the detergent aisle. You can get larger boxes of baking soda at some stores in both the baking section and the cleaning/detergent aisle. For some reason, the boxes that are found in the baking area are cheaper than the ones in the other areas of the store but are the exact same thing.

If you would like to have scented laundry detergent, you can add essential oils of your choice.

To make the detergent, you simply grate the bar of laundry soap and then mix in with all of the other ingredients. Store in a clean container with a lid and carefully label it so you know what it is.

To use your homemade detergent, add one tablespoon of the mixture to a regular or light load of laundry and two tablespoons of detergent for heavily soiled loads.

Fabric Softener Ideas

There are several different things that you can use to soften your laundry beyond the traditional fabric softener products. These include:

½ cup of baking soda added to the washer just before you add the clothes. Allow the baking soda to fully dissolve.

¾ cup to one full cup of vinegar in the wash or rinse cycle

The ultimate softener: ½ cup of vinegar and ½ cup

of baking soda mixed together. When using this you will only need about one half of the usual amount of laundry detergent that you normally use.

This mixture will not only soften your clothes but will help get them much cleaner and will help to reduce static cling in the process.

¼ cup of borax in the rinse cycle will also soften clothes.

Clean tennis balls in the dryer will beat your clothes into softness however they are annoying as they thump about and may also leave an odd smell on your clothes.

There are special little balls designed for this purpose- they can be reused dozens of times and are said to be very effective.

Clothes Freshener

Use this mixture when you need a quick freshening of your clothes but cannot wash them at the moment. You will need:

2 tablespoons of vinegar

2 tablespoons of fabric softener

6-10 drops of an essential oil of your choice or you could use either almond or vanilla extract . Be careful as the oils or extracts could potentially stain your clothes.

Pour into a 16 ounce spray bottle and then fill with water. Shake well before spraying on your clothing.

Snow Can Clean Your Rug!

For those who live where the temperatures dip below freezing and there is plenty of snow on the ground, here is a rug cleaning tip that only requires a bit of elbow grease, a bit of time and some help from Mother Nature herself.

You will need:

About three to four inches of fresh, clean and powdery consistency snow on a very cold day. (Below freezing)

Take your area rug and hang it outside for about half an hour or so. Lay it in the snow, face down and beat it thoroughly with a broom. Flip the rug over and beat the other side in the same fashion.

Sweep the snow from the rug before bringing it back into the house.

The cold will have killed the bacteria and dust mites that might have been in there and the beating will loosen all of the dirt.

Sweeping all of the snow off will have removed all of the loosened dirt and dust mites so your rug is fresh and clean once again.

BONUS

7 Things You Have Probably Overlooked or Forgotten to Clean

Everyone, even the person who is the most fastidious house keeper in the world will have something or another that they forget to clean from time to time.

For instance, some people forget to wipe down the light switches or the door knobs even though these are two of the grimiest and most germ-filled surfaces in your entire home.

Here is a quick checklist to see if you are forgetting any of these grimy culprits:

Behind The Fridge, The Fridge Coils And The Drip Pan

Some refrigerators have sealed coils that do not need to be dusted and cleaned. Others do not.

It is still a good idea to pull it out and give the back side a good cleaning every now and then. Accumulated dust and grime can keep it from working as well as it should and may even hasten its inevitable decline.

You should also take this time to dump the drip pan while you are at it.

Your Make Up Brushes

You put on your makeup- and these things touch your face meaning that they are picking up oils and bits of skin from your face as they go.

Eventually that oil and skin can become a breeding ground for bacteria which is not good.

Every now and then, you should wash your brushes with shampoo and then rinse them with vinegar to kill off any lurking germs.

Under The Bed

If you are from the school of thought that you do not need to move furniture every time you clean, then it is likely that you forget to clean under the bed.

To keep the bedroom as breathing friendly as possible, it is important to eliminate all sources of dust, dust mites and other allergens so that means vacuuming or sweeping under the bed more often than you are currently doing it.

Between And Under The Couch Cushions

If the only time you pull the cushions up is to find the remote control, then you might be missing out on some very interesting treasures. From lost toys to lost earrings to things you could not identify with a CSI lab kit- before one of these little treasures gets a chance to smell up the whole house, you need to eliminate.

Shake the cushions out whenever you clean the living room or whenever you are on a remote hunt and you will keep down the risk of finding something that could either be a very old piece of fruit or your son's missing hamster.

The Grout

No one likes to scrub the grout and the more you resist the more stains and odd colors it will suck up just to spite you. If you clean the grout while you are cleaning the adjacent surfaces, you won't have the rough time that you usually have and it will stay looking better for longer.

Another tip: when you clean it the next time, add a grout sealer and you won't have to clean it for a very, very long time.

The Vent Grates

Every piece of dirt, dust and whatever your vent has is something that can potentially end up flying around the house and breathed in to your family's lungs. All of that dirt can also make your house smell less than pleasant even if it is quite clean.

Don't forget to vacuum the vent grates or wipe them down with a damp cloth. You can also add a drop or two of essential oils to the grate so that when the furnace kicks in there is a subtle, pleasant scent wafted about.

Window Frames

The grooves where the windows are will be the final resting place for all the bugs that were trapped and perished as well as dirt, grime and other disgusting things.

Make sure that you are wiping these areas down- especially when you start closing up the house for the winter and when you start opening the house for summer.

OTHER BOOKS FROM THE BEST SELLING AUTHOR "MATHEW STONE"

PREVIEW OF "DIY HOUSEHOLD HACKS: 40+ Proven Household Hacks To Save Time, Effort, Money And Increase Productivity

INTRODUCTION

Whether you're a new homeowner, or long settled into the responsibilities of maintaining house, there are always smart tips and clever ideas to benefit from.

After all, even the most devoted homemaker doesn't want to spend more time than necessary on chores, right?

Well, in this book, you'll find dozens of helpful hints to keep your home sparkling, with less time spent scrubbing to get it that way.

As a homemaker, I believe that good housekeeping isn't just about cleaning, it's also about neatness and organization, so I've included plenty of ideas that you can use to combat clutter and advance the ever-important cause of tidiness throughout your domain.

No matter what your cleaning and organization approach looks like, whether you're borderline-compulsive or perhaps a bit on the messy side, these **home organization and cleaning hacks** will sure make life much, much easier.

So, in the spirit of getting the most done in the least amount of time, enjoy these great recommendations, and all the cleanliness that's sure to follow!

21 DIY CLEANING HACKS

Hack # 1 – Oily Charm

Greasy buildup, for instance on a stovetop or stove hood, can be the most stubborn and all-around unpleasant mess in your home, so to prove our bona fides, we're starting with the nastiest.

The usual approach for grease is to counteract it with a chemical that can break down its structure—this is how most soaps work—but before you break out the harsh chemicals, try dabbing a paper towel with mineral or vegetable oil and rubbing it into the greasy mess.

Not only will the oils blend, making them easier to wipe away, but also the thin layer of your clean oil left behind will act as a barrier between your stovetop and any new messes.

A similar effect can be achieved with a thin layer of car wax—not only will this make your oven look like a sleek, shiny sports car, but it will also provide a helpful protective coating the next time something spills.

Just apply an extremely thin layer, wipe it down with a soft cloth, and watch as your next mess wipes away with no muss and no fuss.

Hack # 2 – Fun With Fiber

You may not know what microfiber actually is (at least, I sure don't), but if you've had much experience with it at all, you probably know two crucial things.

For one, it's almost unnaturally soft. For two, it's a huge pain to get stains out of.

Well, whatever scientific sorcery went into making the stuff, the key to getting stains out of it is pure chemistry: just spritz the stain with a spray bottle full of rubbing alcohol and then hit it with a white sponge (this will prevent dye from seeping out of the sponge into your fabric).

Then, once the alcohol has evaporated and the fabric is dry, just go over the area with a bristle brush (again, white) to smooth the fibers out. Ta-da!

Click here to check out the rest of "DIY HOUSEHOLD HACKS: 40+ Proven Household Hacks To Save Time, Effort, Money And Increase Productivity"

Or go to: http://amzn.to/1BHncDa

MORE BOOKS BY MATHEW STONE:

Click Here To Download!

Or Go To: http://amzn.to/1xAY6WM

Click Here To Download!

Or Go To: http://amzn.to/1o72ZWN

[Click Here To Read "The Prepper's Urban Guide"!](http://amzn.to/1zkVAI7)

Or Go To: http://amzn.to/1zkVAI7

Printed in Great Britain
by Amazon